ANKYLOSAURUS
AND OTHER ARMORED PLANT-EATERS

Prehistoric World

ANKYLOSAURUS
AND OTHER ARMORED PLANT-EATERS

VIRGINIA
SCHOMP

BENCHMARK BOOKS

MARSHALL CAVENDISH
NEW YORK

DINOSAURS LIVED MILLIONS OF YEARS AGO. EVERYTHING WE KNOW ABOUT THEM—HOW THEY LOOKED, WALKED, ATE, FOUGHT, MATED, AND RAISED THEIR YOUNG—COMES FROM EDUCATED GUESSES BY THE SCIENTISTS WHO DISCOVER AND STUDY FOSSILS. THE INFORMATION IN THIS BOOK IS BASED ON WHAT MOST SCIENTISTS BELIEVE RIGHT NOW. TOMORROW OR NEXT WEEK OR NEXT YEAR, NEW DISCOVERIES COULD LEAD TO NEW IDEAS. SO KEEP YOUR EYES AND EARS OPEN FOR NEWS FLASHES FROM THE PREHISTORIC WORLD!

With thanks to Dr. Mark A. Norell, Chairman of the Division of Paleontology, American Museum of Natural History, for his expert review of the manuscript.

Benchmark Books
Marshall Cavendish
99 White Plains Road
Tarrytown, New York 10591-9001
www.marshallcavendish.com

© Marshall Cavendish Corporation 2003

Cataloging-in-Publication Data

Schomp, Virginia.
Ankylosaurus and other armored plant-eaters / by Virginia Schomp.
    p. cm. - (Prehistoric world)
Includes bibliographical references and index.
Summary: Describes the physical characteristics and behavior of Ankylosaurus and other armored plant-eating dinosaurs.
ISBN 0-7614-1023-6
    1. Ankylosaurus—Juvenile literature. 2. Herbivores, Fossil—Juvenile literature. 3. Dinosaurs—Juvenile literature.
    [1. Ankylosaurus. 2. Herbivores, Fossil. 3. Dinosaurs.] I. Title.
QE862.O65 S4 2002   567.915-dc21   2001043986

Front cover: *Ankylosaurus*   Back cover: *Talarurus*   Pages 2–3: *Saichania*

PHOTO CREDITS:
Cover illustration: The Natural History Museum, London / Orbis

The illustrations and photographs in this book are used by the permission and through the courtesy of:
Marshall Cavendish Corporation: 2-3, 8, 9, 11, 12, 13, 16, 17, 18, 19, 22, 23, 24, back cover. *The Natural History Museum, London:* 20; John Sibbick, 15.

Map and Dinosaur Family Tree by Robert Romagnoli

Printed in Hong Kong
1 3 5 6 4 2

For T.J.

Contents

ARMED AND DANGEROUS

TARCHIA
(TAR-chee-uh)
When: Late Cretaceous,
  80–70 million years ago
Where: Mongolia
• Weighed three tons
• Large tail club of joined
  armor plates

With its heavy armor and huge tail club, Tarchia—*an armored dinosaur closely related to* Ankylosaurus—*had little to fear from hungry predators.*

In the Age of Dinosaurs, a baby *Ankylosaurus* wanders through a lush green swamp. Busy munching on ferns, the youngster is unaware that danger is near. Suddenly a fierce *Tyrannosaurus* attacks. As the giant meat-eater bares its teeth, the baby squeals. Its mother comes charging. Much smaller than *T. rex,* the adult *Ankylosaurus* has a secret weapon—a huge tail club. Swinging her tail, she lands a bone-smashing blow. *T. rex* crashes to the ground. Then mother and baby shuffle off, leaving the wounded giant to the mercy of other predators.

A walking tank. That is one way to describe *Ankylosaurus*. This big bruiser belonged to a group of dinosaurs called ankylosaurs. The ankylosaurs were four-legged plant-eaters with supertough body armor. They lived from about 185 million to 65 million years ago, in the second half of the Age of Dinosaurs. The chart on page 26 shows how *Ankylosaurus* and the other armored dinosaurs fit into the dinosaur family tree.

Euoplocephalus

Edmontonia

The ankylosaurs were armored plant-eating dinosaurs that lived in many parts of the world from the Early Jurassic to the Late Cretaceous periods.

The Age of Dinosaurs

Dinosaurs walked the earth during the Mesozoic era, also known as the Age of Dinosaurs. The Mesozoic era lasted from about 250 million to 65 million years ago. It is divided into three periods: the Triassic, Jurassic, and Cretaceous.

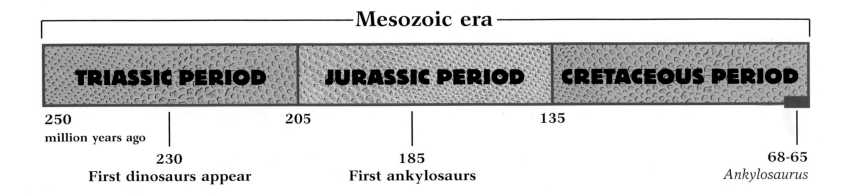

Mesozoic era

| TRIASSIC PERIOD | JURASSIC PERIOD | CRETACEOUS PERIOD |

250
million years ago

205

135

230
First dinosaurs appear

185
First ankylosaurs

68-65
Ankylosaurus

TOUGH GUYS

There were two kinds, or families, of ankylosaurs. Both were covered with thick armor made out of slabs of bone growing right in the dinosaur's skin. One family had a powerful tail that ended in a solid lump of bone. *Ankylosaurus* and the other members of this family could swing their heavy tail clubs like deadly wrecking balls.

Some ankylosaurs had no tail clubs. But many dinosaurs in this family did have long, sharp spikes on their shoulders. A hungry predator would think twice before trying to take a bite out of one of these prickly plant-eaters.

POLACANTHUS
(poh-luh-KAN-thus)
When: Early Cretaceous,
125–120 million years ago
Where: England and Utah
◆ Spiniest armored dinosaur
◆ Two rows of bony triangles
  on tail

Paleontologists disagree over which family of ankylosaurs Polacanthus *belonged to, since this dinosaur had both shoulder spikes and a small tail club.*

ANKYLOSAURUS
(an-kie-loh-SORE-us)
When: Late Cretaceous,
   68–65 million years ago
Where: North America
- Last and largest ankylosaur
- Tail club nearly as large as
  its head

Ankylosaurus *had flexible armor made of hundreds of close-set bony plates, which were embedded in its leathery skin and topped with knobs and spikes.*

TOP OF THE TANKS

The ankylosaurs were named in honor of *Ankylosaurus,* the biggest of them all. As long as a bus and as heavy as an elephant, *Ankylosaurus* moved slowly on strong, stumpy legs. Thick bands of armor studded with knobs and spikes ran all the way from its head to the bony club on the tip of its tail. The only part of this dinosaur's body without armor was its soft underbelly. To a hungry predator, that made a tempting target. But to get to *Ankylosaurus*'s weak spot, an attacker first had to figure out how to flip a four-ton tank on its back!

SAUROPELTA
(sore-uh-PEL-tuh)
When: Early Cretaceous,
115–105 million years ago
Where: North America
◆ Early, primitive
(less advanced) ankylosaur
◆ Teeth in upper beak only

Five-ton Sauropelta *had no tail club but was well protected by armor plates and sharp spikes.*

THE CHANGING WORLD

Armored dinosaurs walked the earth for 120 million years. When they first appeared, in the Early Jurassic period, the earth had one huge super-continent surrounded by sea. The climate was warm and wet year-round. Evergreens, tree ferns, and other plants covered the land like a thick green blanket.

By the days of *Ankylosaurus,* in the Late Cretaceous period, the earth's huge landmass had broken up into large pieces. Rising seas separated

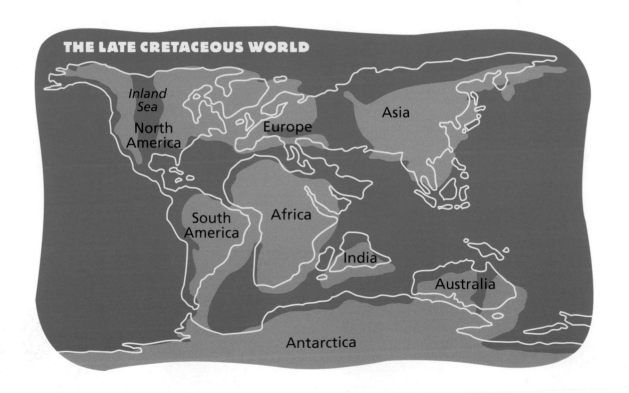

The face of the earth is always changing—but very, very slowly. The yellow outlines on the map show the shape of the modern continents; the green shading shows their position around 65 million years ago, in the days of Ankylosaurus.

these continents. It was still warmer than today, but temperatures were dropping. Seasons began, and flowering plants bloomed. The world was beginning to look much like it does now—except for the strange and amazing creatures that were its masters.

The Late Cretaceous landscape provided armored dinosaurs with plenty of low-growing vegetation to eat, including evergreen shrubs, ferns, horsetails, and moss.

WILD KINGDOM

Let's take a trip back in time sixty-five million years, to the Late Cretaceous period. We land in North America, home of *Ankylosaurus.* The king of the armored dinosaurs lives alongside many other plant-eaters. We might see a herd of peaceful duck-billed dinosaurs. As they gobble up greens, these plant-lovers remain on the alert for predators. Most dangerous of all the meat-eaters is gigantic, fang-flashing, flesh-chomping *Tyrannosaurus.*

Plant-eating duck-billed dinosaurs like this Anatotitan *were the most common land animals of the Late Cretaceous period.*

These meat-eating reptiles—sharp-fanged Kronosaurus *and smaller, long-necked* Cryptocleidus—*roamed the seas when armored dinosaurs walked the land.*

The Cretaceous seas also swarm with wildlife, including fish and immense fish-eating reptiles. Overhead small birds and giant pterosaurs glide. Underfoot small, furry animals hunt for insects. These shy creatures are mammals—our far-distant relatives. One day mammals will dominate life on earth. But for now, the dinosaurs rule.

LIVING DANGEROUSLY

Peaceful *Ankylosaurus* spent most of its time eating. Plodding along with its head bent low, the dinosaur nosed through patches of low-growing plants. Like the other armored dinosaurs, it had an unusually complicated nose, with lots of breathing passageways—perhaps to clean and moisten the desert air, or to make it easy to sniff out food.

> **PANOPLOSAURUS**
> (pan-oh-ploh-SORE-us)
> **When:** Late Cretaceous, 75–70 million years ago
> **Where:** North America
> - Shoulder spikes but no tail club
> - Thick skull with armored eyelids

Panoplosaurus *used its sharp toothless beak to gather up mouthfuls of low-growing, easy-to-chew greens.*

Minmi *was an unusual-looking ankylosaur with bony triangles on its tail and armor all over—even on its belly.*

Ankylosaurus used its sharp beak to nip off soft greens, which it mashed with the small, weak teeth in the sides of its jaw. You wouldn't want to get too close while this dinosaur was feeding. Its huge gut was probably full of bacteria, or tiny living cells, that helped grind up all that vegetation— and also produced incredible quantities of gas.

The armored dinosaurs' plated skin was so thick and tough that some of it has been preserved for millions of years as fossils.

DEADLY DEFENSES

As it lumbered along hunting for greens, *Ankylosaurus* had little to fear. Its strong armor was enough to discourage most predators. In case of attack, ankylosaurs had a variety of defenses. Club-tailed dinosaurs might lash out with their most powerful weapon. A well-aimed whack with a rock-hard club could break the leg of even the largest predator.

Some spiked ankylosaurs might choose to run—not away from an enemy but straight at it. Pointing one spiked shoulder, the dinosaur charged. It must have looked like a cross between a speeding pickup truck and an angry rhinoceros!

If it was too tired or weak to fight, the ankylosaur crouched down. Now its soft belly was protected. Any meat-eater tackling this dinosaur's prickly hide would probably end up with a few broken teeth or claws—and an empty stomach.

A NEED FOR SPEED

Ankylosaurus and its cousins were no speed demons. Toting around all that weight on short, sturdy legs, they usually took life slow and easy. But when they had to, some armored dinosaurs could *move*.

A modern-day four-ton elephant can charge an enemy at twenty-four miles an hour, and a two-ton rhinoceros can run up to thirty miles an hour. A muscular armored dinosaur may have been capable of the same remarkable—and deadly—bursts of speed.

FAMILY LIFE

Paleontologists—scientists who study dinosaurs and other prehistoric creatures—don't know much about the family life of armored dinosaurs. Like all dinosaurs, ankylosaurs hatched from eggs. Babies had small bony plates but no spikes or tail clubs. They probably stayed with their mother until their armor was fully grown.

SAICHANIA
(sie-CHAN-ee-uh)
When: Late Cretaceous,
80–75 million years ago
Where: Mongolia
◆ One of the most heavily armored ankylosaurs
◆ Very complex breathing passageways

With its heavy tail club and armor all over—even on its belly—powerful *Saichania* was well protected against most predators.

TALARURUS
(tal-uh-ROOR-us)
When: Late Cretaceous,
  98–88 million years ago
Where: Mongolia
- About the size of a
  hippopotamus
- Stiff, muscular tail

Talarurus's bony tail club was a powerful weapon in a world prowling with dangerous predators.

Some armored dinosaurs may have lived alone. Others joined together in large groups for protection from predators. When danger threatened, the bigger, older members of the herd may have formed a circle around the youngsters. A wall of angry ankylosaurs—with their built-in armor and weapons—was probably enough to discourage even the hungriest meat-eater.

EDMONTONIA
(ed-mon-TONE-ee-uh)
When: Late Cretaceous,
75–65 million years ago
Where: western North America
♦ Last ankylosaur without a
tail club
♦ Forward-pointing shoulder
spines

Barrel-bodied Edmontonia *lived alongside* Ankylosaurus *until the end of the Age of Dinosaurs.*

END OF AN AGE

*A*nkylosaurus and some of its cousins lived right up to the end of the Age of Dinosaurs, sixty-five million years ago. Then all the dinosaurs died out. Scientists have come up with many possible reasons for this mysterious disappearance—a crashing asteroid, erupting volcanoes, changes in the world's temperature and sea levels. But no one really knows for sure.

We do know that dinosaurs ruled the earth for many millions of years. By studying dinosaur fossils, paleontologists continue to make new discoveries about these amazing creatures. Lots of ankylosaur skeletons and armor became fossils. These ancient treasures hold clues that help scientists bring to life the tanklike tough guys of a long-ago world.

Dinosaur Family Tree

ORDER

All dinosaurs are divided into two large groups, based on the shape and position of their hipbones. Ornithischians had backward-pointing hipbones.

SUBORDER

Thyreophorans were four-legged plant-eating dinosaurs with bony plates and armor.

INFRAORDER

Ankylosaurs were tanklike four-legged plant-eaters with bony body armor.

FAMILY

A family includes one or more types of closely related dinosaurs.

GENUS

Every dinosaur has a two-word name. The first word tells us what genus, or type, of dinosaur it is. The genus plus the second word is its species—the group of very similar animals it belongs to. (For example, *Ankylosaurus magniventris* is one species of *Ankylosaurus*.)

Scientists organize all living things into groups, according to features shared.
This chart shows the groupings of the armored plant-eaters in this book.

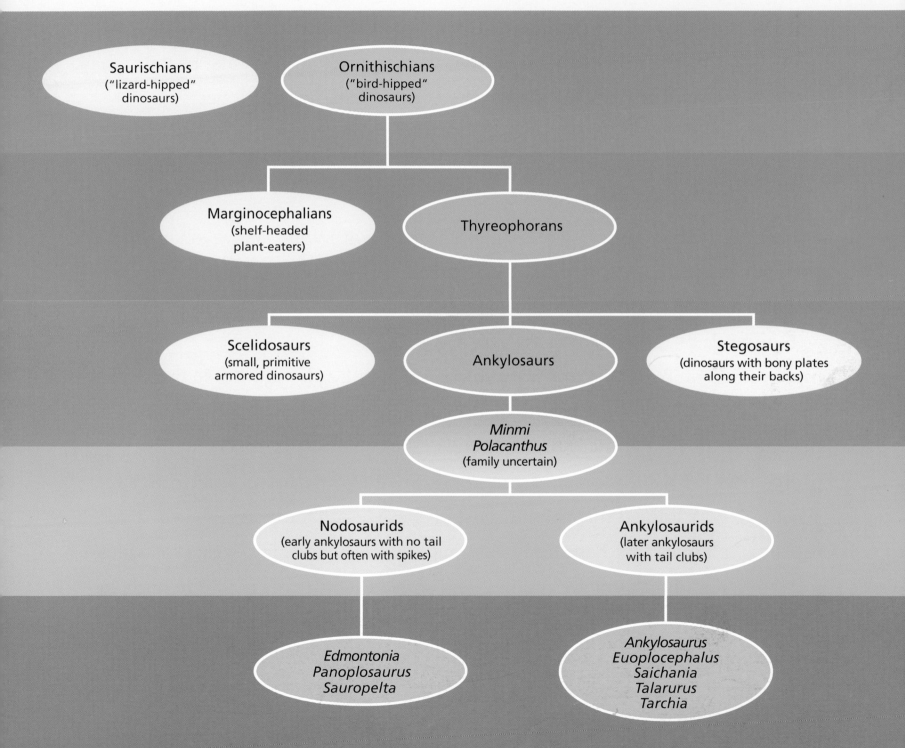

Saurischians
("lizard-hipped" dinosaurs)

Ornithischians
("bird-hipped" dinosaurs)

Marginocephalians
(shelf-headed plant-eaters)

Thyreophorans

Scelidosaurs
(small, primitive armored dinosaurs)

Ankylosaurs

Stegosaurs
(dinosaurs with bony plates along their backs)

Minmi
Polacanthus
(family uncertain)

Nodosaurids
(early ankylosaurs with no tail clubs but often with spikes)

Ankylosaurids
(later ankylosaurs with tail clubs)

Edmontonia
Panoplosaurus
Sauropelta

Ankylosaurus
Euoplocephalus
Saichania
Talarurus
Tarchia

27

Glossary

asteroid: a small planet or fragment of a planet orbiting the sun

bacteria: tiny cells that can live in soil, water, plants, or animals; bacteria may cause diseases or perform useful jobs such as making soil richer

Cretaceous (krih-TAY-shus) **period:** the time period from 135 million to 65 million years ago, when *Ankylosaurus* and the other armored dinosaurs were most abundant

duck-billed dinosaurs: plant-eating dinosaurs with wide, shovel-shaped beaks, which were the most common land animals of the Late Cretaceous period

fossils: the hardened remains or traces of animals or plants that lived many thousands or millions of years ago

mammals: animals that are warm-blooded, breathe air, and nurse their young with milk; humans are mammals

predator: an animal that hunts and kills other animals for food

pterosaurs (TEHR-uh-sores): flying reptiles with wings up to nearly forty feet across, which lived throughout most of the Age of Dinosaurs

reptiles: animals that have scaly skin and, in most cases, lay eggs; crocodiles, turtles, and dinosaurs are reptiles, and some scientists also include birds in this group

***Tyrannosaurus*:** a giant meat-eating dinosaur that was the most fearsome predator of the Late Cretaceous period

Find Out More

BOOKS

Brown, Mike. *Looking at Ankylosaurus.* Milwaukee: Gareth Stevens, 1994.

Dixon, Dougal. *Dougal Dixon's Amazing Dinosaurs: The Fiercest, the Tallest, the Toughest, the Smallest.* Honesdale, PA: Boyds Mills, 2000.

The Humongous Book of Dinosaurs. New York: Stewart, Tabori, and Chang, 1997.

Marshall, Chris, ed. *Dinosaurs of the World.* 11 vols. New York: Marshall Cavendish, 1999.

Parker, Steve. *The Age of the Dinosaurs.* Vol. 10, *Armored Dinosaurs* Danbury, CT: Grolier Educational, 2000.

ON-LINE SOURCES*

Dinorama at http://www.nationalgeographic.com/dinorama/frame.html

Get the latest news on dinosaur discoveries at this National Geographic Society site.

Carnegie Museum of Natural History at http://www.clpgh.org/cmnh

The website of Pittsburgh's Carnegie Museum of Natural History features a 3-D image of the museum's Dinosaur Hall, a fossil slide show, live web cameras, and more.

Kinetosaurs at http://www.childrensmuseum.org/kinetosaur/index.html

Inspired by a traveling museum exhibit of moving dinosaur art, this site sponsored by the Childrens Museum of Indianapolis offers step-by-step instructions for making dinosaur sculptures and other projects. Also includes fact sheets and printouts on *Ankylosaurus* and other prehistoric creatures.

Zoom Dinosaurs at http://www.zoomdinosaurs.com

This colorful, entertaining site from Enchanted Learning Software includes a world of information on dinosaur-related topics: dinosaur myths, records, behavior, and fossils; dinosaur fact sheets; quizzes, puzzles, printouts, and crafts; tips on writing a school report; and more.

*Website addresses sometimes change. For more on-line sources, check with the media specialist at your local library.

Index

Virginia Schomp grew up in a quiet suburban town in northeastern New Jersey, where eight-ton duck-billed dinosaurs once roamed. In first grade she discovered that she loved books and writing, and in sixth grade she was named "class bookworm," because she always had her nose in a book. Today she is a freelance author who has written more than thirty books for young readers on topics including careers, animals, ancient cultures, and modern history. Ms. Schomp lives in the Catskill Mountain region of New York with her husband, Richard, and their son, Chip.